Original title:
Picking Up the Pieces

Copyright © 2024 Swan Charm
All rights reserved.

Author: Linda Leevike
ISBN HARDBACK: 978-9916-89-952-6
ISBN PAPERBACK: 978-9916-89-953-3
ISBN EBOOK: 978-9916-89-954-0

The Graceful Reassembly

From ashes we rise, with hearts reformed,
In the light of His love, our spirits warmed.
Each fragment of faith, a piece of the whole,
In divine hands, we find our soul.

Through trials we walk, in shadows of doubt,
Yet His whispers of hope are what life's about.
Kindness our guide, as we forge anew,
With grace as our anchor, we come shining through.

In community's fold, we gather as one,
Where mercy flows freely, just like the sun.
Together we mend, each heart a strong thread,
In the tapestry woven, no one left for dead.

As seasons may change, and storms come and go,
His promise still stands, through high and through low.
We dance in His light, with joy we embrace,
For all are welcomed in this sacred space.

So let us unite, let our voices resound,
In a symphony sweet, His love all around.
Embracing our stories, imperfect but true,
In the grace of reassembly, we start anew.

Redemption in Ruins

In shadows deep, where hope seems lost,
The weary hearts find gold in frost.
A whisper soft, through ashes calls,
Awakening grace, when the spirit falls.

From brokenness, new strength shall rise,
With every tear, a bond more wise.
In desolation's hold, love's light will bloom,
A promise forged within the gloom.

The Reverence of Reassembly

In fragmented pieces, we seek repair,
A sacred dance, divinely rare.
With every stitch, our souls align,
In trust we place the heart's design.

From scattered hopes to visions clear,
In whispered prayers, our path draws near.
Each moment's thread, a story told,
In reverence we weave, the brave and bold.

Divine Tapestry

In colors bright, the heavens weave,
A tapestry of hope, we conceive.
Each thread a prayer, sewn with care,
In every doubt, divinity's share.

Through trials and trials, this quilt unfolds,
Stories of love and courage bold.
In every weave, God's hand will guide,
Reminding us, we're not denied.

From Despair to Devotion

In deepest valleys, shadows loom,
Yet faith ignites, dispelling gloom.
From aching hearts, devotion grows,
In love's embrace, the spirit knows.

Through every storm, we cling to light,
In sacred stillness, we find our sight.
From ashes rise, our voices blend,
In life's great dance, we transcend.

Healing the Heart's Ruins

In shadows deep, the spirit weeps,
A tender light through darkness creeps.
With gentle hands, the wounds shall mend,
Love's quiet whisper, our true friend.

The rivers flow with grace anew,
Each drop a prayer, each drop a cue.
To rise from ashes, heart aglow,
In faith we stand, through joy and woe.

With every tear, a lesson learned,
In every heart, compassion burned.
The ruins speak, a truth divine,
In brokenness, His love will shine.

Testament of the Shattered

In shards of glass, reflections bare,
We write our lives in grief and prayer.
Each fractured piece a story told,
The strength of spirit, heart of gold.

From depths of sorrow, hope will rise,
Through darkened paths, we claim the skies.
With open hands, we grasp the light,
A testament to faith's true fight.

Though shattered dreams may mark our way,
In every night, there comes a day.
Embrace each flaw, each broken part,
And find the beauty in our heart.

Mosaic of the Faithful

Together we are pieces bright,
In every color, pure delight.
A tapestry of grace is sewn,
In unity, our hearts have grown.

Each broken tile, a tale unique,
In faith we find the truth we seek.
With gentle hands, we form the whole,
In every crack, a sacred role.

The light shines through, a dance of hue,
Each heart a canvas, fresh and true.
A mosaic lived in love and praise,
Together we lift hope's sweet rays.

The Divine Patchwork

Stitched with care, each moment shared,
In threads of love, our hearts are bared.
A quilt of grace, made every day,
In every patch, God shows the way.

Through storms that come, through trials deep,
In faithfulness, our souls we keep.
With each new dawn, a pattern blooms,
In service bright, dispelling gloom.

The fabric holds our dreams and tears,
In every stitch, we face our fears.
A divine patchwork, rich and bold,
In every heart, His story told.

Cherished in the Cracks

In broken paths, His light does gleam,
Amidst the cracks, we find the dream.
Each flaw embraced, His love still flows,
In hidden places, pure grace grows.

As shattered hearts learn how to mend,
In every break, our souls transcend.
From depths of grief, new hope will rise,
Divine design in our disguise.

Sacred Wholeness in Shadows

In shadows deep, where silence hides,
The Spirit stirs, the heart abides.
Wholeness found in what we fear,
In darkness, love begins to steer.

Embrace the night with gentle grace,
In sacred stillness, find His face.
A tapestry of light and dark,
In every shadow, there's a spark.

The Divine Designer's Touch

His fingers weave the stars' bright light,
In every thread, our hopes ignite.
The fabric of our lives unfolds,
In love's embrace, the truth beholds.

With every stitch, a story grows,
Creation's song in whispers flows.
Artistry within each heart's beat,
A masterpiece, divinely sweet.

Breathe Life into Silence

In moments hushed, the breath of grace,
Awakens souls in quiet space.
With whispers soft, He stirs the night,
And turns our silence into light.

In solitude, His glory shines,
In stillness, we hear holy signs.
Breathe deeply now, let spirits dance,
In sacred pause, we find our chance.

Shattered They Rise

In darkness, hope ignites the spark,
In shattered hearts, a light leaves mark.
From broken dreams, a pure heart sings,
In pain, the soul finds the strength it brings.

Each tear a jewel, in faith we find,
From ashes lifted, spirit aligned.
The trials of life, a sacred thread,
In every loss, new paths are bred.

With every stumble, the lessons grow,
Through valleys low, the courage flows.
Like phoenix soaring through the night,
In unity, we embrace the light.

A Symphony of Rebirth

In silence, whispers call us near,
A symphony played for hearts to hear.
Through seasons changing, grace unfolds,
In every heartbeat, the truth beholds.

From winter's chill, to springtime's cheer,
A dance of life, so crystal clear.
Each note of laughter, each tear we shed,
In harmony, all fears are led.

Resilience sings in vibrant rings,
A melody where the spirit clings.
Through trials faced, we rise anew,
In faith's embrace, our dreams come true.

From Ruins to Radiance

In ruins we find our truest form,
In shattered pieces, we weather the storm.
With every crack, the light breaks through,
In darkness met, we gain our view.

From ashes blown, a phoenix cries,
With wings of faith, we claim the skies.
In barren lands, new life can thrive,
From dust to glory, we come alive.

Each step taken, redemption's pace,
In every struggle, seek His grace.
From ruins built, a home we see,
In every shadow, love sets free.

Healer of the Fractured

In every wound, a story spins,
A healer's touch where silence begins.
With gentle hands, the heart mends slow,
In whispers sweet, the spirit grows.

Through trials faced, we find our way,
In love's embrace, we choose to stay.
Each burden lifted, a brighter dawn,
In unity's strength, we carry on.

From brokenness, we learn to soar,
In every fracture, grace restores.
For in the dark, the light shall bloom,
In every heart, there's room for room.

Light Through the Cracks

In shadows deep, the light breaks through,
A whisper soft, from skies so blue.
It warms the soul, ignites the heart,
In every crack, a brand new start.

Through aching nights and weary days,
It guides our path, in tender ways.
With faith as our shield, we rise anew,
In every darkness, light shines through.

A Sacred Symphony of Mending

In harmony, our voices blend,
A sacred song, where hearts can mend.
Each note a prayer, each chord a hope,
Together we learn, together we cope.

The winds of faith, they carry us high,
In the melody, we learn to fly.
With every heartbeat, a promise made,
In this symphony, no soul shall fade.

Prayers for the Pained

We gather here, with hands in prayer,
For hearts that ache, for souls laid bare.
In whispered hopes, we seek the light,
To guide the lost through darkest night.

With every tear, a story shared,
In every plea, the love declared.
United in faith, we stand as one,
For healing grace, our journey's begun.

Seraphic Strands of Healing

From heavens high, the seraphs sing,
Of love and peace, in everything.
They weave the strands of healing grace,
To lift the fallen, to embrace.

In gentle hands, we find our way,
Through trials faced, come what may.
Each thread a promise, soft and bright,
In seraph's song, we find our light.

From Ashes to Blessings

In shadows deep, we find our way,
Through trials faced, we learn to pray.
The fire burns, yet hearts ignite,
From ashes rise, embracing light.

Each tear we shed, a seed of grace,
In emptiness, we seek His face.
Revived by love, we walk anew,
With faith as guide, our spirits grew.

In every loss, a gift bestowed,
The burdens lift, the pain erode.
In silent nights, His whispers call,
From ashes rise, we stand up tall.

The Tapestry of Trials

In the weave of life, each thread a test,
A journey carved, through storm and rest.
With hands entwined, we face our fate,
In trials met, our hearts relate.

Through valleys low, we learn to climb,
Each challenge faced, a path in time.
We rise and fall, yet still we stand,
Guided by grace, a steady hand.

In the darkest night, His light will shine,
In brokenness, His love aligns.
As threads combine, our hopes renew,
The tapestry grows, with colors true.

Embracing Sacred Wholeness

In fractured pieces, we find the whole,
With every trial, a mending soul.
Embracing flaws, we seek His grace,
In sacred love, we've found our place.

With open hearts, we walk the path,
Through storms and grace, we learn to laugh.
In unity found, our spirits lift,
In every moment, we find the gift.

The path to wholeness, a sacred quest,
Each step we take, our very best.
In hands united, we rise above,
Embracing wholeness, a life of love.

The Altar of Restoration

At the altar set, we lay our fears,
With open hearts, we shed our tears.
In brokenness, His peace descends,
Restoration finds, where love extends.

Each prayer a stone, on sacred ground,
In silence deep, His voice is found.
Through every wound, His light can flow,
Rebuilding hopes, where faith will grow.

In gentle hands, our dreams revived,
Through trials faced, our spirits thrived.
At the altar, we come anew,
Restored in grace, our lives imbue.

Blessed are the Broken

In the valley of shadows dim,
The weary find their strength in Him.
He mends the hearts that pain has torn,
With love anew, the soul reborn.

Each tear a testament to grace,
In brokenness, we find His face.
Through trials faced and burdens shared,
The light of hope is boldly bared.

For every wound a story tells,
Of mercy where the spirit dwells.
In whispered prayers, our spirits rise,
In fragile hearts, His glory lies.

So let us gather, hands held tight,
In faith, we walk toward the light.
For blessed are the ones who mourn,
In their embrace, true love is born.

The gentle hands that heal the strife,
In brokenness, we find our life.
Forever grateful, we shall stand,
In the hands of the Divine's command.

Symphony of the Salvaged

From ashes rise the voices sweet,
In harmony, the lost shall meet.
Each note a story, each chord a prayer,
In union found, the soul laid bare.

Rescue resonates through the night,
In darkest moments, find the light.
A melody of hope reborn,
In every heart, His love now sworn.

With hands once empty, now we share,
The symphony of hearts laid bare.
For every crack, the music flows,
In salvaged grace, the spirit grows.

Come join the chorus, voices blend,
With every note, we shall transcend.
In the gathering of the redeemed,
A symphony of love, we're dreamed.

Let every strum and every beat,
Awake the hearts once faced with defeat.
In the song of life, our truths conveyed,
In harmony, our fears allayed.

Graced with Grit

In trials deep, we gather strength,
With weary hands, we go the length.
Through storms and dark, our spirits fight,
With faith, we stand, anchored in light.

Each stumble teaches, each fall refines,
In perseverance, His grace shines.
For in our flaws, His love reveals,
The beauty in the scars, it heals.

The path may twist, the road may bend,
With chaque test, our wills ascend.
In grit we find our purpose true,
The heart's resolve, a faith renewed.

Through hours long and days of toil,
In sacred strength, we till the soil.
For every challenge faced with grace,
Transforms the dust into holy space.

With courage born of trials faced,
In unity, the journey graced.
We're graced with grit, forever bold,
In love, the tales of hope are told.

Celestial Renewal

In dawn's embrace, the world awakes,
From slumber deep, the spirit shakes.
Each day a gift, the sun shall rise,
In celestial renewal, we find our prize.

The stars of night, a guiding light,
In cosmic dance, they shine so bright.
For every end, a new begins,
In heaven's chorus, joy transcends.

The earth rejoices, nature sings,
In every heart, the promise clings.
With every breath, a pledge to bloom,
In grace reborn, dispelling gloom.

Let every moment flow like streams,
In stillness found, we weave our dreams.
For in the cycle, lost and found,
In celestial arms, our peace is crowned.

Awake, arise, let spirits soar,
With gratitude, our hearts restore.
In the sacred dance of life's embrace,
We find renewal in love's grace.

Remnants of Grace

In shadows cast by fleeting light,
The whispers of a hopeful night.
Each heart that breaks, a chance anew,
To find the grace that pulls us through.

Beneath the storm, a quiet song,
A melody that calls us strong.
In every tear, a sacred space,
A glimpse of love, a touch of grace.

Though trials come like raging seas,
We stand in faith, we bend our knees.
In every wound, a story told,
Of mercy's warmth, of hearts consoled.

The dawn will rise, the sun will shine,
And in the dark, His light divine.
So hold on tight, do not despair,
For in our scars, He shows His care.

Let remnants of our past mistakes,
Become the path that true heart makes.
In unity, we search for peace,
In grace's arms, our fears release.

Healing Through Brokenness

In shattered dreams, a seed is sown,
Through trials faced, we're not alone.
Each broken piece, a chance to mend,
In healing light, our spirits blend.

The weight we bear, a sacred gift,
In every tear, our souls uplift.
Through pain we find the strength to rise,
A phoenix born from darkest skies.

In wounds that tell of battles fought,
We find the love that can't be bought.
Each scar a mark of grace bestowed,
In brokenness, our hearts are flowed.

The healing touch of mercy's hand,
Brings solace in the harshest land.
With every loss, a chance to grow,
Through brokenness, His love will show.

We gather all our shattered bits,
In unity, our faith admits.
Together strong, we'll walk this path,
In healing grace, we'll find our last.

The Shattered Vessel

A vessel cracked, yet still it holds,
The light that shines, the truth that molds.
In every flaw, a story clear,
Of grace that flows when hearts adhere.

Though life may break us, we remain,
In shattered forms, we'll bear the pain.
With open hearts, we seek the truth,
In every loss, the face of youth.

The beauty found in fractured seams,
Reflects the hope within our dreams.
For in the cracks, the light breaks through,
A testament of love so true.

The shattered vessel holds the spark,
Illuminating every dark.
In frailty, strength begins to rise,
And faith ignites like morning skies.

In unity, we find our grace,
In every wound, a sacred space.
Together we will stand and mend,
The shattered vessel, love's true end.

Echoes of Redemption

In echoes soft, the heart takes flight,
A whisper from the depths of night.
From ashes rise the spirits bold,
In redemption's arms, our stories told.

With every step along this road,
We carry hope, we share the load.
For in the struggle, truth is found,
In every echo, love surrounds.

Through trials faced and battles won,
We journey forth beneath the sun.
Each scar a mark, each tear a sign,
Of grace that flows through love divine.

In gathering storms, we learn to soar,
Through brokenness, we seek the shore.
And in the quiet, hear the call,
The echoes of redemption's thrall.

In harmony, our voices rise,
Each life a story 'neath the skies.
Together in this sacred dance,
We find redemption in each glance.

Sacred Redemption of Days

Each dawn unfolds a gentle grace,
His light ignites the darkest space.
In whispers soft, He leads us near,
With every step, we conquer fear.

In trials faced, our spirits soar,
Through shattered dreams, His love restores.
A path of hope, a sacred thread,
In faith we tread where angels led.

The sun shall rise, the night must fade,
With prayers sewn, a life remade.
In gratitude, we'll sing His name,
In humble hearts, forever same.

So let us walk, hand in hand,
Along this journey, vast and grand.
Our souls entwined, no fear abide,
In sacred trust, He is our guide.

A Chorus for the Crushed

In shadows deep, the weary weep,
Their hearts are heavy, souls asleep.
Yet from the depths, a voice ascends,
With love and grace, our hope transcends.

The broken sing their mournful song,
In unity, they rise up strong.
Through every wound, His balm is near,
In every doubt, His truth appears.

For in the ashes, beauty grows,
In pouring rain, a garden shows.
A symphony of souls released,
With every note, our hearts increased.

Together we shall forge a way,
With steadfast faith, come what may.
In harmony, our spirits blend,
A chorus sweet, the journey bends.

Fragments of Faith

In shattered glass, a portrait lies,
Each piece reflecting sacred skies.
With every crack, God's light displayed,
A canvas bright, through trials made.

In whispered prayers, our dreams take flight,
A union strong, emerging light.
The world may shift, our hearts shall hold,
In tender trust, His love unfolds.

Though paths diverge and storms may grow,
We find our strength in seeds we sow.
With hearts aligned, we pave the way,
In fragile ties, our hope shall stay.

For faith remains, a gentle guide,
Through every storm, we shall abide.
In every fragment, His truth stands tall,
Together we rise, we shall not fall.

The Divine Mosaic

In pieces small, our lives combine,
A tapestry where love can shine.
Each moment shared, a brushstroke bright,
Creating beauty from darkness' night.

The weaver's hands, so skilled, so sure,
In every thread, His love endures.
Through vibrant hues and muted tones,
A story rich, through hearts and bones.

From joy to sorrow, every hue,
In every shade, His spirit true.
United whole, the fragments sing,
In sacred bond, our hearts take wing.

With every stitch, a purpose drawn,
In quiet strength, we greet the dawn.
Together woven, side by side,
In Divine grace, we shall abide.

Triumph After Turmoil

In shadows deep, faith stands tall,
Through storms that shake, we hear Your call.
With every trial, we find our grace,
In turmoil's grip, we seek Your face.

With tears like rain, the heartache flows,
Yet from this pain, a garden grows.
In valleys low, Your light will shine,
Through darkest nights, our hearts entwine.

From ashes rise, a spirit bold,
In struggle's fire, our souls are gold.
The strength to stand, You freely give,
In triumph's wake, we learn to live.

Regaining hope, we start anew,
In every breath, Your love breaks through.
So let our songs of joy arise,
For we are safe, where freedom lies.

Anointed for Restoration

O Lord, anoint me with Your grace,
Restore my heart, in this holy place.
With faith renewed, I seek Your way,
In gentle whispers, night and day.

Through broken paths, Your light will guide,
In each small step, I will abide.
With hands outstretched, I lift my plight,
And trust in You, my strength and light.

The wounds of past, You heal in time,
With every breath, Your love's a rhyme.
In trials faced, I stand assured,
In Your embrace, I am secured.

In every struggle, joy shall bloom,
Your presence, Lord, dispels the gloom.
I rise renewed, my spirit soars,
Forever grateful, I seek Your shores.

The Journey of Wholeness

In quiet steps, the heart does yearn,
For wholeness found in lessons learned.
With every path, a story told,
In gentle grace, I break the mold.

O guide me, Lord, through trials faced,
In every moment, feel Your grace.
With open eyes, my heart transformed,
In faith I stand, forever warmed.

As rivers flow, so too our souls,
In ebb and flow, we find our goals.
The scars of past, remind us still,
In every journey, find Your will.

Through every storm, Your peace will reign,
In depths of night, release the pain.
With every step, my spirit thrives,
In wholeness found, my heart realigns.

Resurrection of the Broken

From shattered dreams, a cry anew,
In brokenness, I long for You.
With open hands, my heart laid bare,
From depths of sorrow, I find Your care.

O resurrect me, Lord of might,
In darkest hours, You are my light.
The chains of fear, You break and mend,
In every tear, Your love transcends.

These wounds may mark the path I've trod,
Yet in this pain, I seek my God.
Through trials vast, Your strength I feel,
In every bruise, Your love reveals.

With grace unmeasured, hope restored,
From ashes rise, to serve You, Lord.
In every breath, I shall proclaim,
The resurrection found in Your name.

Reclaiming the Lost

In shadows deep, we wander far,
With hearts that chase a distant star.
Each step we take, a plea to mend,
For every soul, a love to spend.

In valleys low where hope may fade,
We seek the light that once displayed.
A hand outstretched, a gentle call,
To lift the broken, one and all.

From ashes rise the dreams of old,
With faith's embrace, we can be bold.
The weary find their paths restored,
In every heart, a silent chord.

Through tears we trace our steps anew,
In every pain, a wisdom grew.
The lost shall find their way once more,
As grace descends from heaven's door.

Together we reclaim the night,
With every shadow, find the light.
In unity, our spirits soar,
The lost are found; we are once more.

The Blessed Fragments

Scattered pieces of the divine,
In every heart, a sacred sign.
Through trials faced, the spirit grows,
In fractured light, our unity glows.

Amongst the shards of dreams once lost,
We find the meaning, count the cost.
In humble faith, we gather near,
In every fragment, love is clear.

The blessed moments grace our hands,
Each gentle touch, like whispered sands.
Through brokenness, our voices rise,
In harmony, we touch the skies.

With every tear, a promise made,
In the unsung, our hopes invade.
Together strong, we seek to find,
The blessed fragments of our kind.

A tapestry of love and grace,
In every stitch, we find our place.
Through trials faced, our hearts expand,
The blessed fragments, hand in hand.

Whispers of the Redeemed

In silent prayers, the whispers dwell,
Of hearts once bound in chains of hell.
Through trials faced, the spirit sings,
In every soul, redemption brings.

From depths of sorrow, hope takes flight,
Each whisper soft, a guiding light.
In gentle tones, the message spreads,
Love conquers all, where goodness treads.

With every breath, the stories flow,
Of grace bestowed, and hearts that grow.
In unity, we find our voice,
In whispered love, we rejoice.

The redeemed rise with spirits bold,
In every heart, a tale retold.
Through narrow paths, the truth we find,
In whispers sweet, we are aligned.

Together we walk, the road ahead,
With every step, we move from dread.
In whispers strong, we shall proclaim,
The love that binds us, in His name.

The Sacred Rebuilding

From ruins deep, we start anew,
With hands of love, we sculpt the view.
Brick by brick, a fortress stands,
In faith we build with guided hands.

The sacred task, a call to rise,
Each stone laid down beneath the skies.
With every choice, we light the flame,
In unity, we stake our claim.

With eyes set high, we face the dawn,
Together strong, a hope reborn.
The walls of doubt shall crumble low,
As love's pure strength begins to grow.

The heartbeat of a new world's song,
In every note, we all belong.
Through trials faced, we shall prevail,
In sacred building, love won't fail.

In every heart a place to dwell,
Rekindled by the love we tell.
For in this journey, we shall see,
The sacred rebuilding, you and me.

The Divine Art of Repair

In shadows deep, the Spirit moves,
With gentle hands, it seeks to soothe.
Through broken dreams and weary hearts,
A thread of hope, the journey starts.

In every crack, a story lies,
Of grace that mends and never dies.
The light of faith begins to shine,
In sacred moments, hearts entwine.

When tears are shed, and burdens weigh,
The love divine will lead the way.
Each fracture holds a lesson true,
And in that pain, we're born anew.

The art of healing, softly kissed,
In quiet whispers, souls persist.
With every stitch, the fabric grows,
A tapestry of grace bestows.

Embrace the scars, they tell a tale,
Of journeys through the stormy gale.
In mending, we discover peace,
As faith unfolds, our fears release.

Restoring the Sacred

Beneath the skies, the sacred we find,
In whispered prayers, a heart aligned.
Through sacred acts, the bonds repair,
In every breath, the love we share.

In nature's arms, the spirit wakes,
Within the silence, guidance breaks.
Each moment held, a chance to heal,
In faithful steps, our truths reveal.

The echoes of the past resound,
In every loss, new hope is found.
Restoration calls, a sacred rite,
To mend what's broken, bring to light.

With hands uplifted, we implore,
For wisdom's touch, forevermore.
In shared communion, we shall thrive,
Restoring soul, the heart alive.

Together joined, a tapestry strong,
In unity, we sing our song.
Each act of love, a force divine,
Through sacred paths, our spirits shine.

Reflections of the Healed

In stillness found, the heart reflects,
On journeys past, the soul connects.
From shattered pieces, beauty grows,
In scars adorned, the Spirit glows.

Each wound a whisper, soft and wise,
A testament of love that ties.
In moments fraught, we learn to soar,
Through trials faced, we seek for more.

The echoes of the healed resound,
A symphony of strength profound.
In gentle light, the truth reveals,
The grace within that softly heals.

With every step, a story told,
Of courage found, of hearts so bold.
The past embraced, the future bright,
In faith restored, we reach for light.

So may we dance in joy and peace,
In gratitude, our hearts release.
For every tear that fell like rain,
Has birthed the joy, has healed the pain.

A Reverent Restoration

In whispered prayers, we lift our cries,
For love that binds, for faith that flies.
And in the silence, grace descends,
A sacred balm that gently mends.

Through trials faced, we find our way,
In reverent hearts, we long to stay.
With every loss, a chance to grow,
In loving kindness, seeds we sow.

Restoration calls, a voice so clear,
In every moment, drawing near.
Through humble acts, we redefine,
A life transformed by love divine.

In unity, we share the weight,
With open souls, we cultivate.
Beyond the scars, a vision bright,
A path of hope, a journey light.

So let us stand, with hands held high,
In faith renewed, we touch the sky.
With every heartbeat, we restore,
The sacred bond, forevermore.

The Alchemy of Affliction

In shadows deep, our spirits soar,
Through trials harsh, we seek the core.
Each wound a mark, a story told,
In pain we find, a heart of gold.

From ashes rise, our faith ignites,
In darkened days, we claim the light.
Transforming grief, a holy flame,
In suffering's grip, we learn His name.

Each tear a prayer, each sigh a plea,
In brokenness, we come to see.
The alchemy of trials faced,
In every loss, a lesson graced.

With every fall, a chance to grow,
Through bitter storms, His love will flow.
Harnessing strife, we persevere,
In sacred depths, God draws us near.

So let us walk, though paths be rough,
In faith we stand, in love we're tough.
For every burden that we bear,
Is woven with a holy care.

Embracing the Crumbled

In shattered dreams, we find our grace,
The broken fragments, a holy space.
Each crumbled piece, a story prays,
In chaos born, we seek His ways.

Amidst the ruins, we lift our voice,
In sorrow's depth, we make our choice.
To embrace the hurt, the lost, the frail,
In love's embrace, we shall not fail.

For every crack, a light shall beam,
In disarray, we build a dream.
With open hearts, we gather all,
From scattered souls, we heed His call.

The crumbling earth, a sacred ground,
In dirt and dust, His love is found.
We gather the pieces, with tender care,
In every sorrow, He is there.

Let us not fear the falling walls,
For in the space, His spirit calls.
Embracing crumpled, we shall rise,
Through brokenness, we touch the skies.

Pillars of New Beginnings

From ruins form, our pillars strong,
In each new dawn, we sing our song.
With faith as stone, and hope as sand,
We build our dreams, with a steady hand.

Through trials faced, we lay the base,
In every heart, we find His grace.
With love as mortar, trust our beam,
In unity, we shall redeem.

Though storms may rage and shadows fall,
Our pillars stand, we heed the call.
For every struggle, a step ahead,
In paths unknown, His light is spread.

We lift our eyes, through dark we see,
In every challenge, we strive to be.
With every breath, a chance to start,
The pillars rise, from broken hearts.

So let us gather, hand in hand,
With faithful hearts, we shall withstand.
For new beginnings, in hand we hold,
With every story, His love unfolds.

Sacred Splinters

In every splinter lies a tale,
Of battles fought, of love's prevail.
Through thorny paths, our spirits bleed,
In sacred splinters, we are freed.

The wood may crack, but hearts aligned,
In brokenness, His grace we find.
With every thorn, a crown is formed,
In suffering's fire, our souls are warmed.

With open hands, we bear our pains,
In every wound, His love remains.
From shattered dreams, new life shall grow,
In sacred splinters, we learn to sow.

So let the hurt be not in vain,
Through every storm, we sing His name.
In splintered wood, we find the key,
To open wide, our destiny.

For in the scars, His love abounds,
In every crack, His mercy sounds.
Embrace the splinters, hold them near,
In sacred depth, He draws us dear.

Mend My Heart, O God

In shadows deep, my spirit weeps,
Where sorrow's weight my being keeps.
Oh gentle Lord, with hand so kind,
Restore the peace that I can't find.

Through trials faced, in darkest night,
Your guiding light ignites my sight.
With every breath, I seek your grace,
Embrace my soul in warm embrace.

With broken dreams and whispered prayers,
I lay my burdens, all my cares.
Mend my heart, O God above,
Fill the void with endless love.

In humble trust, I seek your way,
Within your mercy, let me stay.
Through every storm, your love sustains,
In trials faced, my faith remains.

For in your hands, I find my rest,
A heart once torn, now truly blessed.
O God, my healer, strong and true,
Mend my heart, I cry to you.

In Fragments We Find Faith

In fragments shattered, life unfolds,
A tale of hope, in silence told.
Through cracks of pain, the light shines through,
In brokenness, we find what's true.

Each piece we hold, a story shared,
In every loss, God's love has bared.
With tender hands, we stitch our fears,
In fragments found, we shed our tears.

Together bound by faith's embrace,
We journey on, through time and space.
In shadows cast, our spirits soar,
With faith renewed, we seek for more.

Beneath the weight of worldly strife,
We find the thread that binds our life.
In whispered prayers, our hearts align,
In fragments lost, His love will shine.

So take my heart, O Lord, I plea,
In faith renewed, I long to see.
In fragments true, our spirits grow,
In love's embrace, we're not alone.

The Quiet Heal

In silence deep, the heart can mend,
Where whispered truths and hopes descend.
A gentle breath, a moment still,
In quietude, the soul fulfills.

Beneath the noise of worldly screams,
The heart awakens to its dreams.
In shadows' grace, we learn to feel,
The sacred touch, the quiet heal.

With every tear, a lesson learned,
In stillness found, the spirit yearned.
For in the hush, the purest love,
Descends like blessings from above.

So when the storms of life do rage,
Seek solace in that sacred page.
With faith as anchor, hope as light,
We'll find our way through darkest night.

In quiet moments, hearts unite,
With whispered prayers, we seek the right.
In healing grace, our spirits rise,
The quiet heal, where love complies.

The Sacred Reclamation

In fields once lost, the seeds we sow,
A sacred call, a gentle grow.
From ashes born, we rise anew,
In reclamation, hearts break through.

With every trial, a lesson clear,
The spirit dances, free from fear.
In lands of hope, we claim our place,
With faith as guide, we seek His grace.

From shattered dreams, we build anew,
With every heartbeat, life breaks through.
In sacred love, we find our way,
To light the dark, to usher day.

Through struggles faced and battles won,
The journey's long, but we've just begun.
In sacred reclamation's song,
With spirits pure, we all belong.

So raise your voice, O weary soul,
In unity, we will be whole.
From broken paths, our hearts shall soar,
In sacred truth, we're evermore.

Grace in the Gaps

In moments lost, grace appears,
A whisper soft, calming fears.
Beneath the weight of heavy night,
A spark of faith ignites the light.

Through shadows deep, His mercy flows,
Repairing hearts where sorrow grows.
A gentle hand to guide the weak,
In every silence, He will speak.

When pathways seem to drift away,
In barren fields, He clears the way.
With every stumble, every fall,
He catches us, He hears our call.

In gaps of life, where doubt may reign,
His love remains, our touch from pain.
With open hearts, we learn to trust,
In grace profound, we rise from dust.

In every pause, there's purpose there,
The sacred breath, a holy prayer.
In imperfection, beauty found,
In gaps of grace, His love surrounds.

Embracing Divine Imperfection

In every flaw, a story lies,
A mark of love beneath the skies.
Through broken paths, we learn to see,
Imperfections set our spirits free.

A crack in soil, a chance to bloom,
From darkness springs a sweet perfume.
In tangled roots, His hands reside,
Embracing all, with arms open wide.

Each misstep leads to deeper truth,
In life's mosaic, a whispered proof.
With gentle grace, the heart can mend,
Through every fracture, love will blend.

We find the sacred in the flawed,
A journey rich, our souls applaud.
In the unkempt, in the stray,
Divinity shines, lighting the way.

In every tear, in every scar,
We find our worth, we find our star.
Embracing all that makes us whole,
In divine imperfection, we find our role.

The Light in the Cracks

Amidst the fissures, light breaks through,
Illuminating shadows, soft and true.
In spaces where despair may creep,
The promise shines, our souls to keep.

A world imperfect, yet divinely blessed,
In every crack, His love expressed.
A beam of hope in fractured times,
A secret song in quiet rhymes.

Through brokenness, we find His grace,
Each splintered piece, a sacred place.
In every crevice, joy might spring,
The light within, that makes hearts sing.

When darkness falls and fears invade,
In every shadow, light won't fade.
With open eyes, we learn to see,
The beauty in our mystery.

So let us dwell in light's embrace,
In cracks of life, we find our space.
For in the broken, beauty grows,
The light in cracks eternally glows.

Frayed Threads of Hope

In frayed threads, a tapestry,
Of stories spun, a mystery.
Each knot and weave, a life we share,
In hope we find, we truly care.

With every tear, a chance to stitch,
In trials faced, we find our niche.
A quilt of hearts, both worn and true,
Connected by the love we do.

Through tangled yarns and winding ways,
In every dawn, through every praise,
We gather strength from what's been known,
In frayed threads, we are not alone.

A patchwork made of every pain,
Reminds us of the joy and gain.
With every fray, a chance to mend,
In fragile threads, we find a friend.

So let us weave with tender care,
With frayed threads, a love to share.
In woven hearts, find hope's sweet flow,
In every stitch, our spirits grow.

Fragments of Faith

In shadows deep, a light will break,
A whisper soft, for truth's own sake.
Hearts in anguish, souls to bind,
In fragments of faith, hope we find.

Through trials faced, our spirits sway,
Yet love endures, it lights the way.
With every tear, a lesson learned,
From brokenness, our hearts returned.

Mountains high, and valleys low,
In every step, Your grace we know.
With lifted hands, we seek the dawn,
In fragments of faith, we carry on.

Each prayer spoke, a sacred thread,
Weaving peace where souls have tread.
Though doubts may rise, we choose to trust,
In fragments of faith, rise from the dust.

Together we rise, a chorus sweet,
In every heart, Your heartbeat meet.
With love unchained, we walk as one,
In fragments of faith, our journey begun.

Healing Through Fractures

In every wound, a tale of grace,
Through fractures wide, we find our place.
With gentle hands, You mend our hearts,
In healing, love, our spirit starts.

Each crack a gift, each scar a sign,
Reminders of the love divine.
Through darkest nights, a spark ignites,
In healing through fractures, hope still fights.

From shattered dreams, new visions rise,
You mend our souls, our spirits prize.
Through pain embraced, we learn to see,
In healing through fractures, we are free.

The broken road, a path we tread,
With every step, in love we're led.
From ashes born, a strength revealed,
In healing through fractures, wounds are healed.

Together bound, our voices blend,
In harmony, we learn to mend.
With faith ablaze, we take our stand,
In healing through fractures, hand in hand.

Shattered Altars

Amidst the ruins, prayers arise,
Beneath the skies, our heart's cries.
Each shattered altar, stories told,
In brokenness, we seek the bold.

With lifted hands and weary eyes,
We find our strength in where love lies.
Though temples fall, our faith remains,
In shattered altars, hope sustains.

The rubble sings of lives once poured,
In every crack, a spirit soared.
From ashes gray, new life proclaimed,
In shattered altars, love unclaimed.

Each stone reflects the journey's cost,
Yet from the wreck, no soul is lost.
Rebuilt on trust, we rise again,
In shattered altars, grace will reign.

Together we kneel, and rise anew,
In every heart, a love so true.
With every prayer, we seek the light,
In shattered altars, faith takes flight.

Sacred Whispers

In silence deep, a voice will call,
With sacred whispers, love for all.
In every heart, Your presence dwells,
Through quiet moments, wisdom swells.

Each breath we take, a prayer to soar,
In sacred whispers, we seek more.
With faith entwined, our hopes ignite,
In whispered truths, we find the light.

In shadows cast, Your light breaks free,
A gentle nudge, to set us free.
Through every doubt, Your love persists,
In sacred whispers, our souls exist.

Hearts in yearning, souls in praise,
Each moment cherished, in sacred ways.
Together we listen, a harmony clear,
In sacred whispers, You draw us near.

Through every storm, through every trial,
In sacred whispers, we find our style.
With faith as guide, our spirits bloom,
In sacred whispers, love consumes.

Mosaic of Grace

In shattered pieces, beauty lies,
A mosaic of grace beneath the skies.
Each fragment shines, a story shared,
In every heart, we find the dared.

With colors bright, our spirits blend,
A tapestry where love won't end.
Through brokenness, we weave our way,
In mosaic of grace, we find our say.

From every tear, a prism beams,
Reflecting hope through vibrant dreams.
With open hearts, we dance in trust,
In mosaic of grace, we find the just.

Each hue, each shade, a journey's mark,
In every soul, igniting spark.
Together we stand, and together we embrace,
In mosaic of grace, we find our place.

So gather the pieces, hold them tight,
In unity forged, we seek the light.
With love as the glue, we form our race,
In mosaic of grace, our souls interlace.

Mending the Spirit

In quiet prayer, we seek to mend,
A spirit fractured, our hearts extend.
With gentle hands, we bind the fray,
Through faith and love, we find our way.

The light within begins to glow,
As whispers of grace through shadows flow.
In sacred silence, the soul will rise,
Restoring hope beneath the skies.

Each tear that falls, a lesson learned,
Through trials faced, the spirit yearned.
In unity, we lift each other,
A tapestry woven, sister and brother.

With every breath, we seek the light,
Through darkest hours, we find our might.
In love's embrace, we heal the pain,
Our spirits dance in joyful refrain.

Together we stand, our hands entwined,
In this sanctuary of heart and mind.
The journey long, but worth the quest,
In mending bonds, we are our best.

Sowing Seeds of Renewal

In fields of hope, we sow our dreams,
With faith abundant, we hear the streams.
Each seed of love, a promise made,
In fertile ground, our fears allayed.

The winds of change whisper sweet tunes,
Underneath the watchful moons.
With every dawn, fresh gardens grow,
As life returns, and blessings flow.

We nurture roots with gratitude's care,
Fostering growth through gentle prayer.
In every heart, a flower can bloom,
Dispelling shadows, dispelling gloom.

Together we toil in light and grace,
Finding purpose in this sacred space.
With every step, our spirits gleam,
In sowing seeds, we share the dream.

Through storms we weather, hand in hand,
In unity, we take a stand.
The harvest comes, our souls rejoice,
In every heart, the sacred voice.

The Path of the Restorer

Upon the path where shadows tread,
The Restorer walks, where hope is fed.
With every step, a light shall shine,
To guide the weary, to intertwine.

In valleys low and mountains high,
His gentle whispers lift the cry.
With open arms, He greets our pain,
In brokenness, we rise again.

With hands of mercy, He offers peace,
In every soul, the war shall cease.
Through trials faced, our burdens shared,
The path unfolds, by love prepared.

In circles wide, our spirits blend,
Together we rise, together we mend.
By grace we travel, a sacred quest,
The Restorer's love shall grant us rest.

Onward we go toward brighter days,
In harmony, our hearts ablaze.
Embracing light, we find our way,
Along the path, we choose to stay.

Celestial Reconstruction

In realms unseen, the stars align,
With cosmic threads of love divine.
They weave a tapestry of grace,
In every heart, a sacred space.

With every heartbeat, worlds create,
In unity, we navigate fate.
Celestial whispers guide our hands,
In rebuilding bridges, love withstands.

Amidst the chaos, a melody plays,
A symphony of hope that stays.
In every sunrise, a chance to grow,
To reconstruct all that we know.

Together we soar, we dare to dream,
In the fabric of life, we're never deem.
Through trials faced, the spirit will rise,
In celestial light, our truth never lies.

By faith renewed, our hearts expand,
Stitching the universe, hand in hand.
In every moment, the past reclaims,
A dance of love in sacred flames.

The Lamentations of Renewal

In shadows deep, where sorrows dwell,
A voice of hope begins to swell.
With heavy hearts, we seek the light,
To cast away the endless night.

Tears like raindrops fall in grace,
Each drop a prayer, a sacred space.
From ashes rise, the spirit sings,
Transformed anew, the joy it brings.

O gentle hands, we reach for You,
In brokenness, your love shines true.
With every ache, the path we tread,
Leads softly to the life we're led.

As winter fades to spring's embrace,
The flowers bloom, a holy place.
In grief we find a tender peace,
A promise made, and knows no cease.

Through trials met, our souls refined,
In struggles faced, Your heart aligned.
Each lamentation, a sacred hymn,
In renewal's glow, our faith begins.

Divine Reflection in Shattered Mirrors

In shards of glass, a beauty lies,
Reflections show the truth behind.
Each fragment speaks of life's embrace,
Of broken hearts in sacred space.

We gaze upon our fractured eyes,
To see the pain, the hope that flies.
In every crack, a story's told,
Of love that warms when nights are cold.

O God of grace, we look to You,
In every piece, Your light shines through.
Though life may break, we find the whole,
In shattered mirrors, you mend the soul.

The light refracts, each color bends,
In brokenness, true beauty blends.
Against the dark, your love will glow,
A guiding star, our hearts will know.

In every piece, a lesson learned,
A love that heals, a heart that yearns.
Divine reflection, pure and bright,
In shattered mirrors, we find light.

Battered but Blessed

Though storms may rage and winds may howl,
In trials faced, we humbly bow.
Our battered souls, resilient then,
In every fall, we rise again.

Like storms that bruised, the skies now clear,
A whispered truth, we hold so dear.
In every wound, we find our grace,
With bruised hearts, we seek Your face.

O blessed hands, we cling in hope,
Through darkest paths, we learn to cope.
With every scar, a story shines,
Of battles fought, of love that binds.

In weakness found, Your strength is ours,
In every trial, You raise the bars.
Though battered still, our spirits soar,
In gratitude, we seek You more.

The blessings fall like gentle rain,
Each drop a reminder of love's refrain.
Though battered but, forever blessed,
In faith we stand, and find our rest.

The Bridge Beyond Brokenness

In every heart where sorrow lies,
A bridge of hope begins to rise.
Through valleys low and rivers wide,
We walk together, side by side.

With every step, the wounds we bear,
Are woven tight in love and care.
A path of peace where faith is steady,
In brokenness, our hearts are ready.

O light divine, we seek Your way,
In darkest nights to find the day.
With hands held high, we share the load,
In unity, we walk the road.

The bridge we cross, it bends and sways,
Yet leads us forth to brighter days.
In every crack, your spirit's grace,
Will guide us through this sacred space.

Together strong, we face the storm,
With open hearts, we are reborn.
The bridge beyond, a testament,
To love that heals, a life well spent.

Putting Together the Pieces

In the silence, fragments lay,
Shattered dreams of yesterday.
With gentle hands, He starts to bind,
A tapestry of love defined.

Each piece tells a story bright,
A journey lost, brought back to light.
In faith we trust, in hope we stand,
Together, woven by His hand.

The scars remain, yet serve a plan,
As purpose blooms in the heart of man.
With every stitch, a lesson learned,
In brokenness, the spirit yearns.

What once was lost now shines anew,
In shattered glass, the light breaks through.
He molds the clay with tender grace,
A masterpiece in every place.

So let us gather all the shards,
In unity, we raise our guards.
For in this world, we find our peace,
As we embrace the sweet release.

The Spiritual Artisan

In the quiet of a humble space,
An artisan finds his holy place.
With chisel sharp and vision clear,
He shapes the soul, draws ever near.

Each stroke a prayer, each line a hymn,
In the glow of faith, time grows dim.
He carves with love, each heart a stone,
Creating beauty from the lone.

The marble speaks of strife and grace,
Every flaw, a sacred trace.
In the labor, the spirit sings,
As he unveils what true love brings.

Patience guides the steady hand,
Crafting dreams from grains of sand.
In every piece, a part of Him,
The artisan believes, the light won't dim.

So trust the craft, embrace the toil,
For in His hands, we're bound to spoil.
Each creation tells a story, bright,
In faith, we find our guiding light.

Tending to the Wounded

In the garden where shadows fall,
He tends to hearts, answering the call.
With bandaged hands and gentle care,
He binds the wounds, His love laid bare.

The broken come, seeking His grace,
In quiet whispers, they find their place.
With every tear, a healing rain,
He gathers all, relieves the pain.

Amid the thorns, new life will sprout,
In tender moments, we find out.
That every bruise, a chance to grow,
Restored in love, His light will show.

Wrapped in mercy, no soul too far,
His embrace endures, a shining star.
For in our hurt, His power shines,
A tapestry of love entwines.

So let us walk hand in hand with grace,
In every wound, His love we trace.
Together mending, hearts anew,
In the garden, we're born to bloom.

In the Embrace of Redemption

In shadows deep, a light breaks through,
A promise kept, forever true.
Redemption flows like rivers wide,
With loving hands, He takes our side.

In every heart, a story told,
Of grace bestowed and love untold.
Each sinner's plea, a song of hope,
In His embrace, we learn to cope.

The past may haunt, but fear recedes,
In gentle whispers, He intercedes.
With every choice, a chance to rise,
In His reflection, we claim the prize.

Forgiveness wraps like warmth around,
In His embrace, our peace is found.
The weight of sin forever gone,
In the dawn of grace, we carry on.

So let us stand in faith and love,
With open hearts, we seek above.
In the embrace of all that's kind,
True redemption, forever bind.

Sanctuary in the Shadows

In the stillness of the night,
We find peace in quiet prayers.
Sheltered by faith's gentle light,
Grace whispers through our cares.

Beneath the weight of worldly strife,
Hope blooms like a flower bright.
In shadows, we discover life,
God's presence soothes our plight.

Within the heart's secluded space,
Comfort wraps us like a shawl.
In the dark, we seek His face,
His love, a never-failing call.

Beneath the stars, our spirits soar,
In trust, we lay our fears down.
A sanctuary we adore,
In the shadows, hope is found.

As dawn breaks with golden rays,
We rise renewed, our spirits free.
In each moment, sing His praise,
For in shadows, we can see.

Rebirth Amidst the Ashes

From the ashes, we take flight,
With each tear, a seed is sown.
Darkness fades with morning light,
In His grace, we are reborn.

The fire that once consumed the heart,
Transforms into a sacred flame.
In every ending, a new start,
His love forever remains.

Buried deep within the ground,
In shadows, dreams awaken slow.
In silence, beauty can be found,
From the ashes, life will glow.

Let faith guide us through the night,
For after rain comes the sun.
In His hands, we find our might,
Rebirth has only begun.

With every breath, we rise anew,
A phoenix in the morning light.
In every trial, we break through,
Our spirits take endless flight.

Blessings in Brokenness

In brokenness, we find a way,
To heal the wounds we cannot see.
The heart may ache, but still it may,
Embrace the grace of God's decree.

Through shattered dreams, the light can shine,
In cracks, the hope of love appears.
God's whispers through each fragile line,
In every sorrow, He calms fears.

With open hearts, we learn to mend,
The pieces of our fractured soul.
In unity, our spirits blend,
His love, the balm that makes us whole.

Each tear that falls, a lesson learned,
In trials, we discover strength.
In brokenness, our hearts have turned,
To grace that stretches every length.

Embracing scars, we stand in faith,
For blessings hidden deep within.
In every struggle, find your place,
To rise anew, let love begin.

Echoes of a Fractured Heart

In the echoes of the night,
Whispers of a heart that yearns.
Each beat calls for love's pure light,
As the soul within still churns.

Fractured pieces, scattered wide,
Yet in pain, a beauty grows.
With each tear, the truth does guide,
To the love that gently flows.

In silence, wounds begin to mend,
With patience, healing comes to be.
Every heart has strength to bend,
In His hands, we find our peace.

With grace that dances through the dark,
Hope ignites the yearning flame.
In every ache, a vital spark,
Our hearts' whispers call His name.

As the dawn breaks over the hill,
We rise from shadows of despair.
In unity, our hearts can still,
Echo the love that fills the air.

Sacred Echoes from Ruins

In shadows deep where silence weeps,
Whispers of old through crumbled keeps.
A guiding light in desolate nights,
Awakens hearts to sacred sights.

From ashes rise, the spirit's song,
In every crack, the soul belongs.
The past may fade, yet echoes call,
Through every whisper, we stand tall.

In ruins bare, the seeds are sown,
From broken ground, new paths are grown.
The sacred breath within us flows,
As ancient wisdom gently grows.

Each stone, a testament of grace,
In every heart, a holy space.
From tattered threads, new tapestries,
We weave our faith with hopeful pleas.

So let the echoes guide our way,
Through darkest night, into the day.
For in the ruins, life renews,
In every heart, the truth imbues.

Rebirth from Within

In silent chambers, our souls reside,
With whispers soft, where dreams abide.
A spark ignites, within the dark,
A flame of hope, a sacred mark.

The winter's chill may grip the land,
Yet springs arise by nature's hand.
Through trials faced, the spirit grows,
In every heart, the river flows.

As petals burst from weary trees,
We find our strength upon the breeze.
A journey deep, where shadows part,
The light of life ignites the heart.

Through every wound, the love we gain,
Is too, the balm for every pain.
From depths of sorrow, we ascend,
In every struggle, we transcend.

So let us rise, like dawn's first ray,
Embracing love along the way.
For in the stillness, we shall see,
The rebirth that sets us free.

Healing Hands of Grace

With tender touch, the heart restores,
The healing balm that love explores.
In gentle whispers, peace unfolds,
   A story rich, in warmth retold.

The broken pathways find their way,
As grace descends, a soft bouquet.
In every ache, the strength appears,
In healing hands, we shed our fears.

Through trials faced, we learn to bend,
And in the fray, we find our friends.
With every embrace, the soul's release,
In every tear, we find our peace.

For love ignites the darkest night,
A beacon bright, a guiding light.
With hands of grace, we lift each other,
A sacred bond like no other.

In every gesture, kindness glows,
A stream of hope in gentle flows.
Through healing hearts, the world awakes,
In grace's hands, our journey takes.

Graceful Fractures

In life's mosaic, cracks unveil,
The beauty found in every tale.
From shattered stones, the light gets through,
A dance of flaws, a vibrant hue.

With every fracture, stories rise,
Reflections of our truths and lies.
In brokenness, we find the gold,
A tapestry of life retold.

The graceful lines, all intertwine,
In every fault, the stars align.
Through sacred wounds, the heart expands,
With fragile strength, we make our stands.

For every scar becomes a guide,
In journeys shared, we turn the tide.
Embracing flaws, we learn to see,
The grace in all, the unity.

So let the fractures weave their way,
In every heart, where hope can stay.
For in our brokenness, we find,
The grace that binds all humankind.

The Celestial Craftsman

In skies of azure, He chisels light,
With tender hands, He shapes the night.
Each star a story, each moon a grace,
His artistry whispers in every place.

Through valleys deep, His echoes call,
Guiding the weary, lifting the fall.
With gentle touch, He mends the seams,
Crafting our lives with love's sweet dreams.

The mountains bow to His sacred design,
In the tapestry woven, all hearts align.
Through storms and calm, His purpose clears,
In shadows and light, He calms our fears.

From dust we rise, renewed by His art,
Each breath, a promise, a brand new start.
We walk in faith, with spirits bright,
For the Celestial Craftsman holds us tight.

In quiet moments, we seek His face,
Finding in stillness, boundless grace.
With every heartbeat, we sing His hymn,
In the hands of the Craftsman, we'll never dim.

Pathways of Restoration

In the depths of sorrow, we find the way,
Through shadows that linger, His light will stay.
With every burden, He lifts the load,
Showing the pathways where love had flowed.

The brokenhearted, He binds with care,
In the silence, He whispers there.
Restoring the spirit, igniting the flame,
In pathways of hope, He calls our name.

When despair surrounds like a heavy fog,
He clears the vision, like a morning prologue.
With each step taken in faith's embrace,
We walk on the trails of unending grace.

The lost are found, the weak made strong,
In every journey, we still belong.
Through trials faced, we rise and stand,
Restored by the love of His guiding hand.

Let not your heart be troubled, take flight,
For in His presence, all wrong turns right.
With open hearts, we shall arise,
On pathways of restoration, we reach for the skies.

Faith Forged in Trials

In the fires of testing, our spirits refine,
With each trial faced, we see the divine.
Stronger than steel, our faith takes form,
Amidst the tempest, we weather the storm.

Through valleys of doubt, we journey on,
With faith as our compass, we'll not be withdrawn.
Each challenge a lesson, a step to grow,
In shadows of struggle, His grace will flow.

The path may be narrow, obstacles wide,
But forged in His love, we take it with pride.
With every heartbeat, a whisper of trust,
In the depths of our trials, we rise from the dust.

Courage is born from the storms that we face,
In struggles we find our true joy and grace.
With eyes fixed on heaven, we do not stray,
For faith forged in trials lights our way.

In unity strengthened, we stand hand in hand,
Guided by hope, together we'll stand.
With fire and spirit, our hearts will sing,
For faith forged in trials brings forth the spring.

Threads of Hope

In the fabric of life, we weave our dreams,
Threads of hope shining in golden beams.
Each moment a stitch, each breath, a design,
In the tapestry made, our hearts align.

Through colors of joy and shades of pain,
We gather the fragments, no thread in vain.
With love as our needle, we stitch what's torn,
Creating a quilt where new life is born.

In times of darkness, the threads start to fray,
But hope is the light that brightens our way.
With every heartbeat, we thread with grace,
In the loom of existence, life's sacred space.

Together we gather, united we soar,
In the patterns of trust, we open each door.
With every embrace, we share and cope,
In this grand design, we build our hope.

So let us be weavers, with kind hearts in tow,
For in the threads of hope, we come to know.
Each stitch a promise, each love a plea,
In the quilt of our lives, together we'll be.

Divine Whispers in Shattered Glass

In fragments of the soul they speak,
Soft whispers echo, tender and meek.
Each shard a voice of love divine,
Guiding the heart where hope will shine.

Amidst the chaos, grace unfolds,
In cracks of life, a story told.
The light breaks through in radiant beams,
Transforming pain into sacred dreams.

With every piece, a truth revealed,
In brokenness, the spirit healed.
The glass may shatter, yet still we rise,
Embracing love beneath the skies.

Our hearts, though tattered, find their place,
In shattered glass, we see His grace.
Through trials faced, our faith ignites,
In fractured beauty, we find the light.

So let the whispers guide our way,
Through broken paths, we choose to stay.
For in the shards, God's presence glows,
In shattered glass, His mercy flows.

Resurgence through Faith

In darkest hours, Our hope awakes,
With faith as guide, Our hearts it takes.
Through storms of doubt, we stand as one,
Embracing grace until it's done.

Each trial faced, a chance to grow,
With every tear, Our roots will sow.
In ashes rise, the spirit's flight,
Resurgence blooms from darkest night.

The mountains high will bend their knee,
As faith endures, we rise and see.
Through valleys deep, our souls will soar,
In unity, we seek the shore.

With faithful hearts, we lift our song,
In love's embrace, where we belong.
Resurgence through the trials we face,
With every breath, we find His grace.

Together strong, we move ahead,
In faith we trust, and fear we shed.
Resurgence glorious, light to share,
In every heart, His love laid bare.

The Blessing of the Broken

In every wound, a blessing lies,
A tender touch from heavens high.
In brokenness, we find our strength,
In moments lost, we find our length.

From shattered dreams, new hopes arise,
Like starlit skies at dawn's surprise.
Each crack a path to deeper grace,
In broken hearts, we seek His face.

To bear the scars, a badge of love,
Each pain a gift from God above.
For in our trials, we are blessed,
In brokenness, His heart confessed.

The broken bread, a sacred gift,
In every heart, the spirits lift.
With grateful hearts, we raise the song,
The blessing found where we belong.

Oh, let us dance in ashes' glow,
For through our fray, His love will flow.
The blessing of the broken, bright,
In every shadow, shines His light.

A Journey of Restoration

In valleys low, the path unwinds,
A journey forward, love reminds.
With every step, we seek the light,
In stories woven, wrongs made right.

Through seasons change, our hearts will learn,
With every ache, a bright return.
In whispers soft, we find our peace,
Restoration comes, our fears release.

In every heart, a sacred call,
To rise anew, we stand not fall.
Our spirits dance amidst the fray,
Restoration leads the weary way.

With every tear, a purpose found,
In each of us, His love is crowned.
Through trials faced, we pave the road,
In journey's end, His grace bestowed.

The path may twist, but never break,
With faith as guide, we choose to wake.
A journey blessed, in Him we grow,
Restoration's light, forever glows.

The Wholeness Within

In silence, the spirit finds its call,
A whisper of truth beyond the thrall.
With faith we gather, in stillness abide,
Embracing the light that dwells inside.

Every breath a prayer, a sacred trust,
Within our hearts, the sacred must.
The journey unfolds, both gentle and grand,
In unity, we stand, hand in hand.

Through shadows we walk, yet never alone,
For love is the key, a steadfast tone.
In the depths of despair, hope brightly shines,
Reveal the wholeness in the divine signs.

Each heartbeat a testament, each tear a grace,
In the arms of mercy, we find our place.
Together we rise, with each loving prayer,
In the tapestry woven, our souls are laid bare.

In the fabric of faith, let courage ignite,
Awakening wonder, dispelling the night.
We journey within, where the sacred aligns,
The wholeness we seek, in the truth brightly shines.

Revival from the Remains

From ashes we rise, a phoenix anew,
In the wreckage of sorrow, life's beauty breaks through.
With hands that are willing, we start to rebuild,
Reviving the hope that our hearts once filled.

The pain is a teacher, its lessons so clear,
In shadows of loss, the light will appear.
Every fragment of faith, a promise in time,
With grace as our guide, we shall surely climb.

Voices now echo, a symphony strong,
In the chorus of love, we find where we belong.
Together we gather, like rivers unite,
Revival is birthed in our shared light.

Each struggle a stepping stone back to grace,
In the embrace of community, we find our place.
With hearts opened wide, we carry the flame,
Reviving the spirits, never the same.

Through trials we've wandered, and storms we've sown,
In the garden of life, seeds of hope have grown.
Together we flourish, with love as our aim,
Revival from remains, forever our claim.

Anointed to Fix the Fractured

With oils of compassion, we gather to heal,
The wounds of the world, our hearts they reveal.
In the quiet of prayer, our spirits align,
Anointed with purpose, we're lovingly defined.

Each crack that we see, a story unfolds,
In the light of His mercy, our mission is told.
With grace in our hands, we mend what is torn,
For the broken are cherished, the lost will be borne.

In unity, strength, we rise to the call,
To lift up the weary, to stand and not fall.
With voices uplifted, together we'll sing,
Anointed to fix, we embrace every being.

In the heart of the city, where shadows may creep,
We'll walk with the fragile, their promises we keep.
Each life is a candle, together they glow,
Fractured yet beautiful, together we grow.

The love that we share, a balm to the soul,
In the art of mending, we find ourselves whole.
Anointed to fix, with compassion we core,
In the symphony of life, we rise evermore.

The Patching of Belief

In the tapestry woven, our doubts may entwine,
With threads of conviction, their colors define.
Through moments of darkness, we seek the repair,
The patching of belief, a fabric so rare.

With hearts wrapped in faith, we gather as one,
In the warmth of each other, we find a new sun.
The patches we stitch, each story a guide,
In the fabric of grace, our dreams coincide.

Through storms of uncertainty, we stand resolute,
In the crafting of hope, our spirits take root.
Where rips have been sewn, new patterns emerge,
The patching of belief, a beautiful surge.

In the circle of love, we share our refrain,
With patience and kindness, we cherish the grain.
Each thread tells a story, each knot holds a key,
In the patching of belief, we are truly free.

Together we flourish, our spirits entwined,
In the art of believing, our hearts are aligned.
With every new stitch, a promise we weave,
In the patching of belief, we learn to believe.

Reverent Reconstruction

In the depths of silence, prayers rise,
Hearts mend beneath the heavens' skies.
Faith gathers fragments, hopes entwine,
Building altars where love aligns.

Each tear a testament, echoing grace,
Restoration unfolds in this sacred space.
Hands joined in reverence, souls ignite,
A tapestry woven with divine light.

From ashes we rise, strong and bold,
New beginnings born from stories told.
In unity's embrace, we find our way,
Reverent hearts shall not lead astray.

In every heartbeat, the spirit flows,
Finding strength in the love that grows.
Together we stand, no longer apart,
Reconstruction of faith, a brand new start.

With each step forward, we trust the path,
Finding joy in the journey, escaping wrath.
Like the phoenix, our spirits soar,
In reverent reconstruction, we seek for more.

From Shattered Dreams to Holy Visions

In the wake of night, dreams decay,
Yet hope whispers softly, leading the way.
From broken pieces, visions arise,
Painting the darkness with radiant skies.

Through trials and storms, we learn to see,
The beauty in fragments, setting us free.
With faith as our compass, we journey on,
Transforming our grief to a new dawn.

Each heartache lingers, a tale to tell,
In the sacred silence, we find our well.
From shattered dreams, we craft with care,
Holy visions emerging from despair.

Guided by spirits, the lost have found,
In unity's embrace, our souls unbound.
The light that once flickered now brightly beams,
From shattered dreams, we build new dreams.

In every heartbeat, a song of grace,
From darkness to light, we find our place.
With every step forward, faith lights the way,
From shattered dreams to holy visions, we pray.

The Anointed Fragments

In the quiet embrace of grace divine,
We gather the fragments, a sacred sign.
Each piece anointed with love's sweet breath,
Woven in faith, transcending death.

From sorrow's shadows, we rise anew,
Healing the wounds with love so true.
Each fragment holds stories, whispers of light,
The anointed fragments, guiding our sight.

In unity's chorus, we sing our song,
Together in spirit, where we belong.
Every heart intertwined, no longer torn,
In our anointed beings, hope is reborn.

With hands uplifted, we honor the past,
In the love of the future, forever steadfast.
Fragment by fragment, we stitch our ways,
Creating a quilt of infinite praise.

Let the anointed guide us on high,
Through valleys of shadows, beneath the sky.
Each moment a treasure, life's sacred art,
In the anointed fragments, we find our heart.

Holy Harmony in the Helix

In the spirals of life, where spirits entwine,
We seek the harmony, so pure, divine.
Each twist and turn, a lesson to learn,
In holy rhythm, our souls yearn.

In the helix of hope, we rise and we bend,
Finding the beauty in every end.
With faith as our anchor, we dance in the light,
Holy harmony shining so bright.

The universe whispers, a cosmic refrain,
In every heartbeat, we feel the same pain.
Yet love unites us, a celestial bond,
In the helix of life, we are endlessly fond.

With every twist, our spirits align,
In the sacred embrace, the stars intertwine.
Guided by love, we rise above strife,
In holy harmony, we find our life.

Through trials we wander, but never alone,
In the helix of grace, our true selves are shown.
Together we sing, let our voices soar,
In holy harmony, forevermore.

Saints Among the Splinters

In the quiet whispers of the wood,
The saints reside where shadows stood.
Here in the cracks, their grace unfolds,
In stories of love that light the cold.

Each splinter speaks of trials faced,
Of faith and hope, in dreams embraced.
They gather close, in humble prayer,
Guiding our hearts through dark despair.

With every mark, a lesson learned,
Divine embers of passion burned.
They teach us still to rise each morn,
In splendor dressed, from pain reborn.

The tides may rage, the winds may howl,
Yet voices call from every vowel.
In unity, our spirits soar,
Together strong, forevermore.

So let us walk, where they have tread,
In sacred paths, where truth is spread.
For in the splinters, wisdom flows,
A haven found, where love still grows.

Reconstructing the Soul

In the shattered pieces of our plight,
Lies the spark of hope, a silent light.
With gentle hands, we mend the cracks,
Faith like mortar, never lacks.

Each fragment sings of trials past,
Of promises made that forever last.
Through whispered prayers and softened tears,
We build anew, dispelling fears.

The heart once broken finds its way,
Through guided love, we learn to sway.
With every breath, the soul takes flight,
In the embrace of the holy night.

Touched by grace, reborn to live,
A testament to all we give.
In unity, we find our strength,
Embracing life in fullest length.

So let us gather, hand in hand,
Together we'll rise, a faithful band.
For in reconstruction we will see,
The beauty of divine mystery.

Visions from the Fragments

In shards of dreams, reflections gleam,
Visions arise, like a fleeting stream.
Through broken paths, the light will guide,
Journeys deep where souls abide.

Each piece a story, woven whole,
In sacred order, they make us whole.
Through eyes awakened, we will see,
The tapestry of destiny.

Winds may howl, and storms may rage,
Yet hope remains on every page.
In whispers hushed, we hear the call,
To rise anew, to never fall.

Bridges built from remnants lost,
In faith we stand, despite the cost.
With every heartbeat, we reclaim,
The essence of our spirit's flame.

So let us walk with hearts aglow,
In fragments, love will always flow.
For every vision brings us near,
To unity, our purpose clear.

The Light That Mends

In the dawn of hope, a light appears,
Chasing away the darkest fears.
With every ray, the heart renews,
In sacred love, the spirit brews.

Through trials faced and paths we tread,
The light that mends, where shadows led.
With gentle guidance, we find our way,
Embraced by grace in the light of day.

In every struggle, a lesson shown,
The seeds of kindness gently sown.
In the warmth of faith, we find our stand,
Together united, a healing hand.

So let the light shine on our hearts,
In unity, where love imparts.
For every fracture, every bend,
Can find its peace, the light that mends.

With spirits bright, we rise and soar,
In the presence of love, forevermore.
For in this glow, we find our role,
The light that mends, the holy soul.

Transcendence in Turmoil

In shadows deep, our spirits stray,
Yet light shall guide the weary way.
Through trials fierce, the heart will glow,
In clamorous storms, His love we know.

From whispers soft, to thunder's roar,
He reaches down from heaven's door.
In every bruise, a lesson learned,
In chaos' dance, our souls discern.

When faith feels lost, we seek the spark,
In darkest nights, He lights the arc.
Though tempests rage, and doubts invade,
In turmoil's grip, His peace is made.

With every tear, a prayer ascends,
To Him who heals, our broken bends.
Through anguish wrought, we rise anew,
In trials' forge, we're made so true.

So take our hands, O holy guide,
In unity, we shall abide.
From churning seas to shores divine,
In turmoil's heart, His love will shine.

The Holy Art of Reconstruction

When ashes fall, and dreams decay,
He whispers hope, shows us the way.
With hands divine, He crafts the clay,
In each fracture, new paths to play.

From broken hearts, emerge the whole,
In every wound, He reclaims the soul.
The canvas waits for His embrace,
In His great light, we find our place.

With faith, we gather scattered parts,
In His great love, the truth imparts.
Though storms may blind our tearful eyes,
In rebuilding grace, our spirit flies.

He lifts our gaze, through shadows thick,
With every beat, His pulse we pick.
In ruins bare, our hopes align,
The holy art of love divine.

So let us rise, unite and sing,
For in His hands, we're everything.
Through reconstruction, strong we stand,
In gentle grace, we walk His land.

Wholeness from Wounds

In every scar, a story lies,
Of battles fought, of whispered cries.
Yet from the hurt, the heart will bloom,
In tender grace, dispelling gloom.

He takes our sorrows, turns them gold,
In trials faced, the brave unfold.
From shattered dreams, new visions seed,
In every wound, there's life indeed.

For brokenness is not the end,
But pathways where the spirit mends.
In sacred light, our shadows blend,
And through the pain, we will transcend.

Each tear a pearl, every quake a song,
In wholeness found, we all belong.
From ashes rise, and learn to dance,
In every fall, embrace the chance.

Together bound, we heal the earth,
In every wound, we find rebirth.
For in His love, our spirits soar,
Wholeness from wounds, forevermore.

Ascending from the Abyss

From depths so dark, where shadows creep,
The soul awakens from its sleep.
With every breath, we rise again,
In grace bestowed, we shed the pain.

Through valleys low, our faith ignites,
In whispered prayers, we find the light.
With every step, the chains will break,
In hope reborn, no more to ache.

The journey long, yet hearts will yearn,
For in the trials, wisdom earned.
We seek the fire that burns so bright,
That guides our hearts to heaven's height.

With open arms, the heavens call,
To rise from depths, to stand tall.
In unity, our spirits blend,
From abyss deep, His love will send.

So take the leap, relinquish fear,
For He who loves is always near.
From dark to light, the promise clear,
In faith we trust, our path is sheer.

Milton Keynes UK
Ingram Content Group UK Ltd.
UKHW031321271124
451618UK00007B/165

9 789916 899526